BATS

A PORTRAIT OF THE ANIMAL WORLD

ANDREW CLEAVE

TODTRI

This book was designed and produced by
TODTRI Book Publishers
P.O. Box 572, New York, NY 10116-0572
FAX: (212) 695-6984
e-mail: info@todtri.com

Printed and bound in Singapore

ISBN 1-57717-130-6

Author: Andrew Cleave

Publisher: Robert M. Tod
Senior Editor: Edward Douglas
Photo Editor: Linda Waldman
Book Designer: Mark Weinberg
Typesetting: Command-O Design

PHOTO CREDITS
Photo Source/Page Number

Theo Allofs 52, 53

Peter Arnold, Inc.
John Cancalosi 59
Stephen J. Krasemann 49
Arnold Newman 54 (top)
Hans Pflietschinger 27
Michael Sewell 51
Günther Ziesler 6, 34 (top)

BBC Natural History Unit
Jim Clare 46 (top)
Hans Christoph Kappel 5, 71
Dietmar Nill 17 (bottom), 33 (top), 42 (top), 67

Joe McDonald 4, 10 (bottom), 12 (top), 29 (bottom), 55

Photo Researchers, Inc.
Stephen Dalton 8–9, 29 (top), 30, 33 (bottom), 35, 39, 40–41, 45
Ken Highfill 62
John Mitchell 56–57
Morley Read 34 (bottom)
Gregory K. Scott 21
Merlin D. Tuttle 7, 12 (bottom), 14, 17 (top), 22, 23, 28,
31, 36, 41 (right), 42 (bottom), 44, 46 (bottom), 47, 48,
60 (top), 61, 63, 64 (bottom), 65, 66, 68–69, 70
Larry West 24–25, 26

Merlin D. Tuttle 3, 10 (top), 11, 13, 15 (top & bottom),
16, 18 (top & bottom), 19, 20, 32 (top & botom), 37 (top & bottom),
38, 43, 50, 54 (bottom), 58, 60 (botttom), 64 (top)

INTRODUCTION

The hairy slit-faced bat is recognized by its strange facial features. Unusually among bats and other mammals, it has a tail with a T-shaped tip. These bats are found in Africa and Asia.

T*he secret, nocturnal world of bats is a mysterious, rather sinister one to most people; bats are generally misunderstood, if not actually feared, in most parts of the world. Legends associated with bats are usually frightening, involving blood sucking, witchcraft, and sorcery. People are convinced that bats will spread diseases, damage the woodwork in their houses or fly into a lady's elegantly coifed hair. The silhouette of a bat seen against the night sky somehow grows in people's imaginations so that bats are thought to be creatures large enough to attack domestic pets.*

Once introduced to bats, however, most people are won over and quite happy to share their homes with them, often becoming protective about these previously despised species. Most of the bats encountered by people living in towns and cities are very small, and when people see how small and vulnerable they are, and realize that they are tiny, furry, warm–blooded mammals, they no longer fear them.

A VARIETY OF SPECIES

There are about 900 different species of bats in the world, and they show a great variety of different forms and behavior patterns. Everyone can recognize the basic structure of a bat, which is common to all the known species. However, they have evolved many different body forms that have helped them to occupy a great variety of niches, and live in most parts of the world except the very cold polar and high altitude regions.

Bats can range in size from the giant fruit bats with wing spans approaching 6 feet (2 meters) to small insect eaters with bodies only just over 1 inch (3 centimeters) long. Some of the heaviest bats may weigh in at over 2 pounds (1,000 grams) but the smallest may be only around 1/15th ounce (2 grams), making them the lightest weighing mammals in the world. Most bats have a body covering of hair, but this too is subject to great variation; it is usually plain brown or gray, but some are white, some have stripes, and some seem to have no hair at all.

The diet of bats is also quite variable and can include fruit, pollen and nectar, fish, frogs, lizards, small mammals, or insects. Each type of food requires a specialized method of feeding, and it is this which has given rise to the great range of body forms and some very odd adaptations.

There is one feature which is common to most bats, and that is their nocturnal habits. During the day most will roost in some secure hiding place, safe from predators and avoiding competition with other mammals and birds. At night, when most birds and mammals have retired, the bats have all the food to themselves, and they can feed without fear of predators or competition.

Classifying Bats

The scientific name for the bats is the Chiroptera—an order, or group within the mammals. The name Chiroptera means "hand

A greater mouse-eared bat, one of the largest of the Microchiroptera species, displays the full-membraned tail in hunting flight.

Flying foxes are the largest of the bats and very widespread in tropical regions where the warm climate and readily available fruit supplies provide them with ideal conditions. Unfortunately, many species, such as this very large one from India, are becoming scarce, due to habitat loss and persecution.

The fruit-eating bats are important pollinators of many tropical plants. This Peruvian banana flower is especially adapted to be pollinated by bats, hanging downwards to deter other mammals or birds, and yielding most of its nectar and scent at night when the bats are active.

wing" and refers to the structure of a bat's wing, which, although it serves the same purpose, is quite different from a bird's wing. The Chiroptera are divided into two sub-orders, the Megachiroptera, which are the large fruit bats, and the Microchiroptera, which are the smaller, mainly insectivorous, or predatory species.

There are about 165 species of fruit bats, or flying foxes, as they are sometimes known, and they are mostly found in Africa and eastward as far as some of the Pacific islands. Most species have dog-like faces with large eyes and large, widely separated ears. Most species have claws on the second digit as well as the thumb. Males are larger than females. Eyesight is used to aid navigation as only a few species are able to use echolocation. Coat color is generally uniformly dull brown, but

there are a few colorful species like the Rodriguez flying fox which can have black, light gray, yellow, and orange coat colors. Males of some species have other colors that are used to effect in courtship displays. A number of the more gregarious species live in colonies of hundreds of thousands. The cave-dwelling rousette fruit bats live in vast colonies and may have to fly considerable distances at night to find enough food.

Wahlberg's epauletted bat licks its lips after eating a tasty fig, a typical meal for this large fruit-eating bat. The dog-like face, with its large eyes and relatively small ears, is typical of the Megachiroptera, or flying foxes. The eyes are the most important sense organs in this order of bats.

An Indian fruit bat, or flying fox, shows the dog-like face typical of these large bats. Fruit bats are becoming endangered due to habitat destruction, and most species are highly sensitive to disturbance of their roosts.

Kitti's hog-nosed bat perches on a rock; this species was not known to science until 1974. It is the world's smallest mammal, measuring no more than 1.2 inches (3.3 cm) long, and weighing little more than 1.8 ounces (1.5 gm) It is found in bamboo forests and plantations in Thailand.

A little brown bat in typical resting posture. Not all species conform to the popular idea of bats hanging from cave roosts; many prefer to conceal themselves in crevices or cling to trees.

Microchiroptera

The Microchiroptera are sub-divided into a number of smaller groups, classified according to their body structure and habits.

The mouse-tailed bats are recognized by their body-length, exposed tails, and small size. They occur in arid and associated dry agricultural areas and often roost in ancient temples and similar buildings; the species found in Egypt uses crevices in some of the pyramids.

The sheath-tailed bats, found throughout the warmer regions of the world are among the smallest of all species and are recognized by the short tail which projects a little way out of the tail membrane. Some males have wing sacs that release an odor thought to be attractive to females.

Kitti's hog–nosed bat is the smallest bat in the world and was only recognized as a species in 1974. It is confined to a cave in Thailand, where only a very small population survives and is in need of special conservation measures.

The slit-faced bats, found in Africa and nearby regions of Asia, have a complex facial structure in which the nose leaf is divided by a groove running as far as a pit between the eyes. A further unusual feature is the tail with a T-shaped tip. They are mainly insectivorous, living in caves and large buildings.

The head of the lesser mouse-tailed bat shows features more typical of the Microchiroptera, or echolocating bats. The eyes are small, but the ears are large and complex. The nostrils are surrounded by leaf-like folds, and the mouth is equipped with tiny teeth for feeding on small insects.

A short-tailed leaf-nosed bat, widespread across Central and South America, raises its wings in rapid forward flight.

False vampire bats are large bats with populations ranging from Africa and India to Australia. The ears are large and usually joined on top of the head, and the eyes are also large. Since most are capable of taking large prey like birds and small mammals, feathers, fur, and bones litter the ground under their roosts.

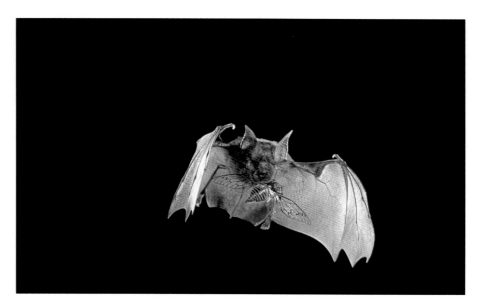

A horseshoe bat makes a successful kill. It is not always easy for the bat to capture large insects, as some are able to detect the ultra-sounds emitted by the bats and take avoiding action at the last minute.

Horseshoe bats gained their name from the curious horseshoe-shaped nose leaf. The ears are large and pointed and usually have no tragus (a fleshy prominence at the front of the opening of the ear). They are very maneuverable in flight, due to their broad wings, and fly with their heads pointed downward, not forward as in most bats. They are insectivorous, roost in caves and buildings, and are found in Europe, Asia, and Japan.

Leaf-nosed bats are similar to the horseshoe bats but are generally larger with a less-well-defined nose leaf. Most feed on large insects, but some may take small vertebrates. A few roost in vast colonies in caves. They are found in the tropics from Africa and Southeast Asia to Australia.

Leaf-chinned bats are found in the southwestern United States, Central America, and much of South America. They lack a nose leaf, but the lips are extended to form a dish-shaped structure. Some cave roosts support immense numbers of bats whose droppings are mined as a form of fertilizer.

Returning to its roost with its prey, the false vampire will suspend itself from its hind feet, fold its wings, and use its powerful teeth to deal with a small bird.

The false vampire is America's largest bat, but as its name suggests, it is not a true blood-sucking species. Despite its menacing appearance, it is no threat to animals larger than itself. However, it can still take quite large prey.

The false vampire, a very large bat with a powerful flight, preys on small birds and mammals, locating them in the dark by echolocation and by the sounds they emit themselves.

Dobson's horseshoe bat, from Southeast Asia, has elaborate "nose leaves" typical of all the horseshoe bats. These large bats are highly skilled at locating and capturing large, fast flying insects.

A spear-nosed bat may not be the most attractive mammal in the world, but its extra-ordinary facial features suit it to a life of echolocating in the dark. The sounds emitted by the bat are reflected off objects around it and picked up by the large ear lobes.

The extra large ears of the California leaf-nosed bat help it pick up the echoes of the ultra-sounds it emits to help locate its prey. The ears are protected by extra flaps of tissue, known as a tragus.

The Mexican bulldog bat is highly skilled at flying over water at night, and makes many successful dives on fish near the surface. The long claws and the tail make effective fish-catching apparatus.

The bulldog bats are noted for their fishing skills and have specially adapted toes to enable them to grip small fish in flight. The teeth and lips are designed to secure slippery prey. They will take insects if fish are not available. Two species are found in Central and South America.

The small short-tailed bats are confined to New Zealand and nearby islands and are small insectivorous species. They have extra projections on their thumbs and claws and use these to help scramble around on the ground and excavate hollows in rotten trees. They feed on a range of food, including insects, nectar, and pollen.

The spear-nosed bats are a large family of about 140 species found from southwestern United States to Argentina. They generally have a spear-shaped nose leaf and fairly simple

The funnel-eared bats are very small, delicate bats which feed on very tiny insects detected by echolocation, using extremely high frequency ultra-sounds. They are found in Central and South America and many Caribbean Islands.

Since the true vampire bat takes the blood from large mammals as they sleep on the ground at night, it must come down to the ground itself to locate them, sometimes adopting unusual postures as it approaches its intended victim.

ears. Most are insectivores, but some of the larger species take other bats, small reptiles, amphibians, and birds. They use a variety of roost sites from caves to trees, and some are tent builders, sheltering in large leaves.

Vampire bats are found in Mexico and South America. Specially adapted teeth, lips, and tongues allow them to cut into the exposed skin of a sleeping mammal and drink a small quantity of blood. The common species prefers mammals, but two rarer species usually prey on birds.

Funnel-eared bats occur in Central and South America and many of the Caribbean islands. They are small bats with long slender wings and funnel-shaped ears. They emit some of the highest frequency sounds of all bats, which they use to find tiny insects. It is thought that they estivate, that is, go into torpor in the summer, rather than hibernate.

Thumbless bats are found in tropical South America and are very small. Thumbs are present but functionless. Little is known about them apart from their cave-roosting habits and insectivorous diet.

Disk-winged bats are small species found in the tropical forests of South America. They have specially adapted suckers to enable them to roost on smooth surfaces like Heliconia leaves.

The sucker-footed bat from Madagascar is a very rare species with suction discs on its wrists and ankles which are apparently functionless.

A pair of tiny Spix's disc-winged bats shelter in a rolled leaf. Found in the tropical forests of Central and South America, these bats have suckers on short stalks attached their wings and legs, that help them grip smooth leaf surfaces for roosting.

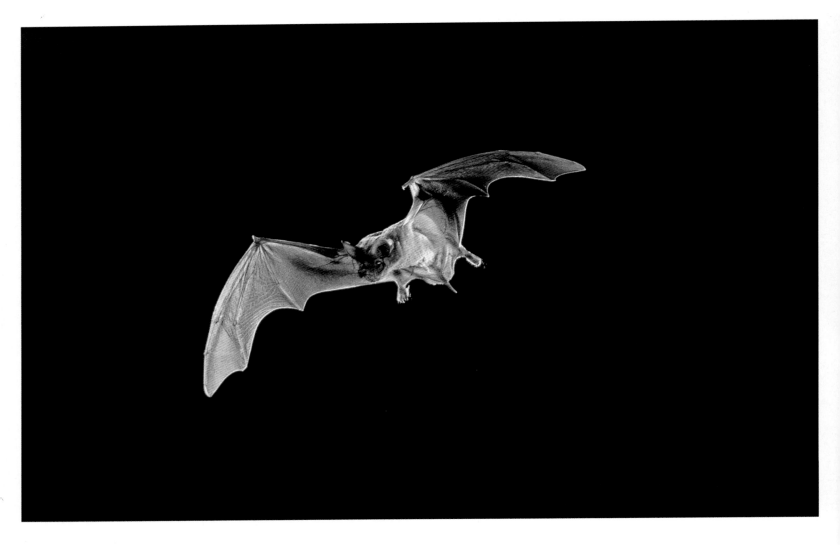

A Mexican free-tailed bat in flight shows the thin, hairless projecting tail. This is an unusual feature, since most bats normally have the tail incorporated into the wing membrane.

The common, or vesper, bats are the most widespread family, found everywhere except for the polar regions and very high altitudes. One genus, *Myotis*, is the most widespread mammal genus after *Homo sapiens*. Most are insectivorous, but many other diets occur. Cave roosts are popular, but trees and human habitations are also used; the spread of humans has allowed some species to increase their range by providing man-made roosts in otherwise treeless or cave-free areas. These are the bats which most people are likely to encounter in towns and cities.

Free-tailed bats are found in sub-tropical and tropical regions from the southern United States to Argentina, southern Europe, Africa, Asia, and Australia. Most are small to medium sized bats, distinguished by the exposed tail projecting beyond the membrane. Wings are long and narrow to aid fast flight. This family includes the so-called "naked" bats that have a thick, black skin and pouches into which the wings are folded when the animal at rest. The nursery colonies of the Mexican free-tailed bat hold the greatest numbers of bats, or indeed of mammals, to be found anywhere, with estimates of 50 million individuals using them at times. Some species are known to migrate for distances of up to 800 miles (1,300 kilometers).

Most bats are insectivorous, taking a variety of small flying insects from mosquitoes to large moths and beetles. Their sharp teeth are able to grip them and break through insect cuticles. The North American big brown bat, seen here hiding in a rock crevice, is a large bat, capable of feeding on tough insects like beetles.

BAT ANATOMY

Bats are mammals with all the typical mammal features, such as a covering of body hair, the ability to produce live young and suckle them with milk, and a constant body temperature. The body temperature, however, is subject to variation. For example, bats living in temperate regions have the ability to hibernate, thereby lowering their body temperature to just above freezing point.

Most bats have a covering of body hair, which is often quite dense and provides good insulation. For the very small bats this is extremely important since it is far more difficult for a small mammal to maintain a high body temperature. The surface area of the body is large in relation to the volume, so heat is lost rapidly. A thick covering of fur helps greatly with insulation, as does roosting communally and folding the wings over the body when at rest.

The thick fur of the red bat provides it with excellent insulation, enabling it to live in temperate regions where summer temperatures may not be very high.

Wahlberg's epauletted fruit bat has returned to its roost with a large ripe fig, a highly nutritious source of food. Its large eyes and small ears are a contrast to the facial features of the smaller insectivorous bats.

FOLLOWING PAGE:
A North American red bat tackles a large beetle on a leaf. This species has beautifully soft, thick red fur and a pale underside. It hibernates in hollow trees and is tolerant of temperatures down to freezing point.

Hair and Coloration

The hair itself is quite distinctive if viewed under a microscope. Each hair has a covering of thin scales, which makes it efficient in providing insulation. It is also quite long in comparison with the hair of other small mammals. Some of the tiniest bats, such as the pipistrelles, would look incredibly small without their fur coats, since the long, scaly hairs tend to fluff up and increase the apparent size of the bat. In some of the larger species, such as the flying foxes, the hair has a more conventional structure, but these large animals do not have the same problems of heat conservation.

Most bats are fairly uniformly colored, in shades of gray, black, or brown, with paler buff or light gray areas below. A few tropical species may show stripes or patches of different color, but for a nocturnal mammal, colors and patterns are not very important. Bats communicate with each other mostly by scents and sounds, rather than with visual signals such as markings, so colors generally serve to camouflage them when roosting.

In most species the hair has two or more colors along its length, and the bat may appear to be multi-colored if the hair is ruffled up or has become wet. Young bats have grayer colors than adults, and their fur is usually softer and more downy until they have undergone their first molt, when they take on the colors of adults.

Grooming is very important to bats, and a long time is spent every day combing through the coat with one foot while hanging upside down by the other. Parasites are removed in this way, and knot and tangles are unraveled, leaving the coat sleek and smooth. Molting takes place once a year, in a very gradual process, so that worn and damaged hairs are regularly replaced. Fast-flying species usually have very sleek coats, but the slow flyers have thicker, more ruffled coats. Thicker coats are more commonly found in the colder regions.

Wing Structure

The wings are the bats' most striking features, separating them immediately from other

The extended wings of a large mouse-eared bat illustrate the formation of the limbs. The wing membrane is stretched across the fore and hind limbs, and over the tail, but the hind feet and the thumbs of the front limbs are left free.

The hoary bat is noted for its thick fur. It is also a migratory bat and is known to fly over long distances. It has been able to colonize the Hawaiian Islands by flying up to 2,300 miles over the Pacific Ocean.

mammals. They are formed from the extended bones of the hand. An X-ray of a bat's wing shows a very similar arrangement of bones to that in a human's hand, but with long, thin fingers that are almost as long as the bat's body. The fingers are connected by a thin skin which also connects with the hind legs and the sides of the body. This delicate membrane is almost hairless and is usually brown or black; if held up to the light the outlines of the internal skeleton can be see. The four fingers of the hand are normally contained within the membrane, but the thumb is detached. The membrane is easily damaged, so bats are very careful to avoid contact with objects such as thorny twigs which might break it. Small holes usually heal over, and these show as flesh-colored scars. Larger rips and tears may not repair themselves completely, but just heal over at the edges. Depending on the severity of the tear, the bat will still be able to fly, but with reduced efficiency.

The shape of the wing varies from species to species according to the lifestyle and habits of the bat. Fast flyers generally have longer, narrower wings than slow flyers. Flying is hard work, so the bat will usually try to launch itself from a high perch, dropping into the air to build up speed before flying properly. Bat wings differ from bird wings in being solid structures that do not allow air to pass through them. This helps them to make rapid twists and turns in the air far more efficiently than birds can. Very slight differences in the positions of the fingers will help the bat execute these turns. High speed flight is important to some species and speeds of 30 miles-(50 kilometers-) per-hour have been recorded for many of the insect catchers. Variations in the shapes of the wing are seen in bats, and these are related to the speed of flight and the maneuverability of the bat. Long, thin wings are best for rapid flight, while shorter broader wings are better for rapid twists and turns.

A long wing span is essential for fishing bats, enabling them to glide successfully over open water, and then pull away safely when the prey has been grasped.

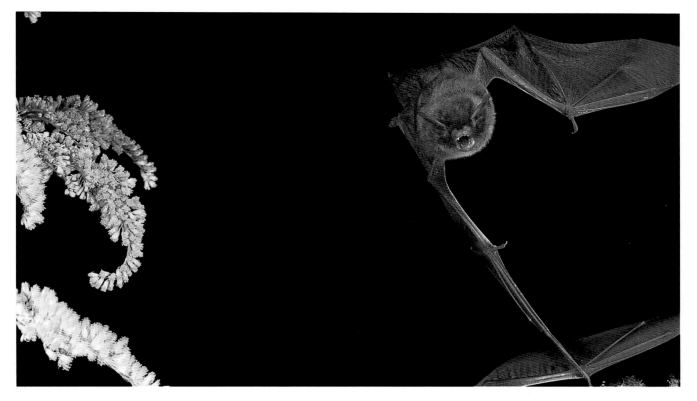

A little brown bat shows its remarkable agility in the air. It can make rapid twists and turns, avoiding twigs and branches that might damage its wings, while pursuing insects in the dark.

Why Do Bats Hang Upside Down?

The elaborate wing structure, perfectly suited to flight, means that the front limbs are no good for anything else. This only leaves the hind legs for movement on the ground, scrambling in crevices, or hanging on perches. The hind limbs have specially arranged tendons that close the toes when pressure is exerted on them. Sharp claws give a good grip on small crevices and perches, and the weight of the bat tightens the tendon to close the grip. Once the bat has hung on to its perch, it can sleep quite happily without any fear of falling off. This is the posture adopted for short breaks and sometimes for longer periods of sleep, but bats will also roost in crevices and other tight spots where they can rest their bodies on a support. The claws on the ends of the thumbs will also be used for extra grip.

Hanging from the roof of a cave or the rafters of a barn keeps torpid bats away from predators when they are in a very vulnerable condition, but they will also use horizontal crevices if these are safe enough. Where space is at a premium and the colony of bats is large, some bats will hang on to other bats, but somehow they will all manage to sleep securely.

Tails

Most bats have tails as long as their bodies, but they are not very obvious since they are often incorporated into the wing membrane. At rest, it is usually curled under the body. In flight, it is extended and serves a number of functions. It helps with aerial maneuvers, including braking, and in some species it is used to carry insect prey while the bat is still feeding. A few species have "free" tails that are not incorporated into membranes.

A successful hunt ends with the capture of a large insect. Note how the tail is used to prevent the escape of the prey. The mouse-eared bat will take its prey away to a safe roost to eat it.

An African leaf-nosed bat chews on a large cricket. Bat roosts can often be identified by the litter of undigested insect remains, such as legs and wings, that collect on the ground beneath favorite feeding areas.

A vampire bat glides through a South American forest at night, wings outstretched and mouth open as it echolocates. The thumbs can be seen clearly; these are used to help it maneuver itself when on the ground.

A fisherman bat rests on a log after a successful swoop on a small fish. The prey is normally taken to a safe riverside roost so that it can be maneuvered into the best position for swallowing.

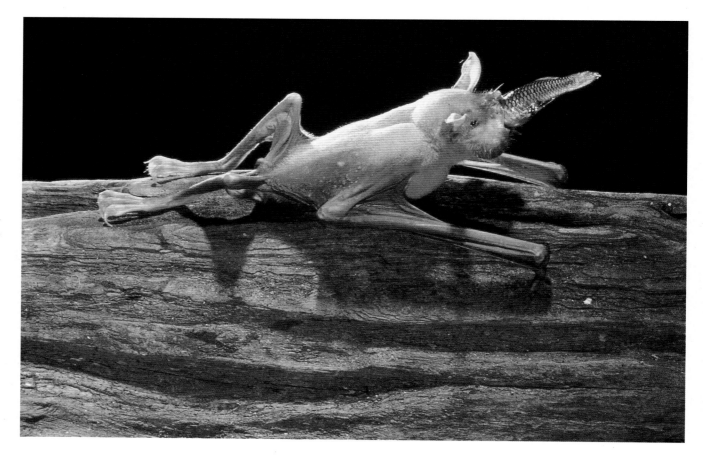

A Bechstein's bat locates a moth hiding under a lime leaf. Like many species, this European bat is skilled at finding prey in woodlands and among dense foliage, and can pluck an insect from a perch as it flies.

The elegant flight pattern of a fishing bat reveals how the feet and tail are used to make the capture. Fishing bats are able to locate their prey by detecting minute ripples on the water's surface.

A vampire bat from Argentina reveals its sharp teeth that are used to slit open the skin of sleeping mammals. The eyes are relatively large in this species.

Teeth

Newly born bats have "milk" teeth, but these are soon replaced by their permanent teeth whose structure is suited to the bat's method of feeding. Milk teeth are quite sharp and hooked in some species. They may help the baby bat hang on to its mother while she is flying around with the baby beneath her.

Insect feeders have very sharp molars, or cheek teeth, used for crushing insects, as well as pointed canines, designed to secure and grip live prey. The incisors, or front teeth, are normally very small in insectivores, and when a bat's mouth is open, it looks as if it has no front teeth at all. Bats are unable to bite pieces out of their food, so it has to be passed to the side of the mouth and chewed with the molars, rather in the fashion of a dog chewing a bone.

Fruit eaters have large, powerful molars for crushing fruits and seeds, and strong jaw muscles to help cope with tough foods.

A fruit-eating bat from Trinidad shows the large teeth suited to cutting open the skins of large fruits, and the large hind feet which are used to grip the fruit; they often use one foot to bring the fruit close to the mouth. Not visible here are the flattened back teeth which can crush fruit pulp and small seeds.

Sharp teeth, and large, powerful jaws allow this false vampire bat to seize a live mouse. The bat's swift silent approach does not give the mouse enough time to make its escape.

As Blind as a Bat?

Contrary to the popular myth, bats have good eyesight. The large fruit bats, or flying foxes, have very large eyes and good night vision, but even the smaller insectivorous species have good eyesight. They do not have color vision, but that is not a problem for a mammal that hunts at night, when colors would not be visible anyway. Bats' eyes are suited to low light levels and are good at detecting shapes and movement. They use their eyes to determine if it is dark enough to safely leave their roosts and start feeding. They also need to be able to find their roost site and feeding territory.

Sense of Smell

Bats use their sense of smell to find out about other bats. Many species have scent glands which release odors used to mark roosts and each other. This could be important in large colonies when mothers leave their young to go off to feed, and then need to locate them among many others when they return. The scents are usually not distinguishable by humans, but in large colonies an accumulation of the scent may give a residual musky odor. If a bat is handled, it may sometimes release large amounts of scent which adhere to surfaces, including human skin, and will persist for some time. Some tropical bat species have scent glands on the face and chest and at the base of the tail.

Hearing

Bats have very sensitive hearing, and for most species, this is a very important sense. They are able to detect very high pitched sounds that are far beyond the range of human hearing, and most species are able to produce high

The horseshoe bats, such as this large Asian species, show some of the most elaborate facial developments of all bats. The nose-leaves aid the amplification and direction of the ultra-sounds, and the large ear lobes help pick up faint echoes from the sounds as they bounce back from their prey.

"As blind as a bat" is not a very accurate description, for all adult bats, like this big brown bat, have functioning eyes, even though their sense of hearing is actually more important to them.

The sense of smell is very important to most bat species, and the nostrils are well developed. Although bats primarily hunt by using echolocation, they use scent for other purposes, particularly communication with others of their own species.

pitched sounds as well. They are sensitive to disturbance at their roosts, and can pick up sounds made by rustling clothes and squeaking shoes, as well as the faint sounds made by some insects.

Echolocation

Their method of locating food and learning about their surroundings in the dark has enabled bats to occupy a niche not available to other mammals or birds. Echolocation involves emitting very high-pitched sounds and then listening to and analyzing all the echoes that return from the surroundings. The echo will return immediately from very close objects, but take longer to come back from harder surfaces farther away. It will be louder if

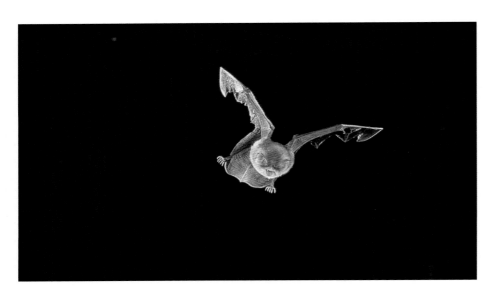

A Mexican funnel-eared bat hunts tiny insects using very high-pitched echolocation. Its wings are prepared for the final swoop on its prey.

it comes from something close and will also be much more clearly defined if it is from a solid material like the wall of a building. Moving vegetation will give an indistinct echo while a moving object will give a trace of echoes. By analyzing all of these sounds and textures, the bat will be able to build up a sound picture of its surroundings; it will be able to judge distances and textures from the quality of the echoes it receives. When seeking food, bats emit a series of sounds, like short yelps, at great rapidity, sometimes as many as ten a second. If the sound returns from a slightly different position after each call, then the object is moving and may be an insect which can be taken as food.

The calls are inaudible to the human ear, but can be made audible by the use of an electronic "bat detector;" this picks up the bat's calls and converts them into a sound audible to humans. It is possible to distinguish between different species by studying the different frequencies, rhythms, and durations of calls they emit.

Some species fly high and in open areas, so they emit loud calls at relatively long intervals; there are fewer obstacles for them to collide with, but they need loud calls because the echoes have farther to travel. Other species emit very quiet sounds. It is possible that these quiet sounds are a ploy to outwit the few moth species that are able to hear the bats calling. The moths that can locate bats usually drop to

safety just before the bat swoops in to make a capture, so the quiet calls may not be detected. The bats with the quiet calls usually have very large ears in order to pick up the equally quiet echoes. The long-eared bats, that whisper rather than yelp their calls, have ears almost as long as their bodies.

Many of the sounds emitted by bats are very complex, and even with the aid of the bat detector, can not be fully interpreted by the human ear. Some sounds are emitted in incredibly short pulses, often at the rate of dozens a second. The bat detector will produce a sound like an insect buzzing, but if the call is recorded and then slowed down, the complex structure of the call will become more obvious.

Some calls are emitted on a single frequency, while others start at a high pitch and drop down to a lower note. The bat detector will usually pick up this kind of call at one frequency only, so not all of the call will be heard. The bats with very quiet calls will probably not be picked up at all unless they are very close. The bat detector is invaluable at picking up bat calls, but interpreting the calls requires considerable skill and experience. Several species may be calling at the same time, some species can vary their calls according to conditions, and some may call at a frequency beyond the range of the detector.

In addition to their ultra high frequency calls, bats also make various chattering and squeaking sounds that are audible to humans. Some species are particularly vocal at their roosts, especially when the time approaches to emerge. A crescendo of chattering usually means that bats are about to leave the roost. More angry buzzing sounds are sometimes heard when bats are disturbed at their roosts, and there are occasional audible squeaks from frightened baby bats.

A mouse-eared bat, one of the largest European species, homes in on a perched insect which it will capture in its mouth as it swoops past. Many species specialize in picking insects off foliage, and sometimes locate them by their calls.

STRATEGIES FOR SURVIVAL

About one third of the world's bats are fruit eaters, while most of the rest are insect eaters. Of these, the great majority take insects on the wing at night. Most insectivorous bats specialize in one type of insect; the smallest bats generally taking the smallest insects. Large species with powerful teeth can tackle night flying beetles and crickets, while the majority take moths. If bat droppings are examined, they are usually found to contain the indigestible remains of insects in the form of legs, wing cases, and scales. Sometimes these can be matched against live specimens to help identify the bat's prey.

A lesser false vampire bat from the Khao Chong Pran cave in Southeast Asia, captures a large moth, one of the commonest prey species for night-flying bats. The moth is showing the warning coloration on its hind wings.

A long-nosed fruit bat prepares to land on a bird-of-paradise flower. The long lower bract on the flower makes a convenient perch during feeding.

Pallas's long-tongued bat maneuvers its way between large branches in a forest in Costa Rica in search of night-scented passion flowers so that it can feed on nectar. The passion flower depends on the bat for successful pollination.

The long-nosed bats possess extra long tongues, often with bristly papillae near their tips. With these, they are able to reach into flowers and fruits while hovering near them, and eventually withdraw, covered with nectar and pollen.

The spear-nosed bats visit flowers for nectar, and in the process, transfer pollen as they move from flower to flower. Many plants are totally dependent on bats for pollination; a decline in bat numbers can seriously affect the plants' seed production.

Hunting

Bats hunt in areas where insect prey is likely to be concentrated, so woodland edges, night-flowering shrubs, ponds and marshes, and street lights are frequently chosen. Bats often hunt in groups, congregating in areas of abundant food. Many species use regular flight paths in their feeding areas, patrolling regularly along the same route until they establish that no more food is present.

The ideal weather conditions for hunting insects are when the nighttime temperature remains above 50° F (10° C), the air is damp, and there is no moon. Insects tend to seek cover when there is a bright moon—presumably because of the risk of predation—and avoid spells of very heavy rain. Bats also avoid very heavy rain because the water reduces the insulating properties of the fur.

Small insects are usually captured in the open mouth, but larger ones may be scooped up by the tail membrane and then transferred to the mouth. The wings may sometimes be used to flick an insect towards the mouth.

A false vampire bat, one of the largest predatory species, flies off with a mouse, an easy prey for this very powerful nocturnal predator.

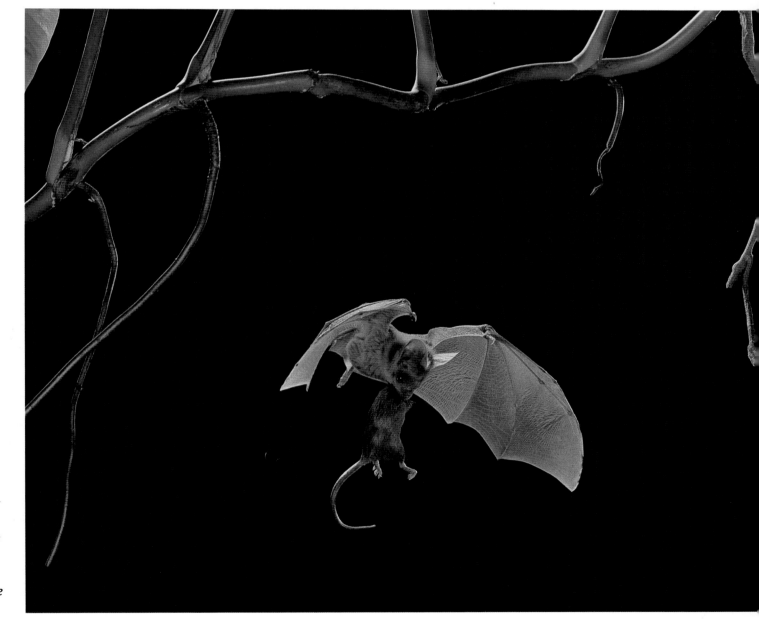

Niceford's forest bat consumes a large cricket. It is more energy efficient for the bat to take a few large prey items than expend energy flying around the forest at night in pursuit of large numbers of very small insects which have very little food value.

45

Much of the time spent away from the roost at night will be occupied by feeding and some species will consume enormous quantities if it is available. Checking on body weights of bats before and after going out on a night-time foray has shown that some individuals are able to increase their body weight by as much as 25 percent. Insect food normally passes through the digestive tract fairly quickly, so some of the food caught may already have been processed before the bat returns to its roost.

A body-weight increase of these proportions indicates a very large number of insects. A colony of bats will dispose of vast numbers between them over the course of a summer season. Many of these will be troublesome species of night-flying insects like gnats and mosquitoes, or potentially damaging ones like wood-boring beetles, so insectivorous bats perform a very useful service.

Resting on the ground, an Argentinean vampire bat sucks blood from the flipper of a young sea lion. The vampires normally make their incisions in areas of thin or soft skin where capillaries run close to the surface. Their delicate bites are usually not noticed by sleeping animals.

The dramatic climax to a hunt as a frog-eating bat from Barro Colorado Island, Panama, snatches a frog from the water in a dramatic swoop.

*A frog-eating bat from Barro Colorado swoops in for the kill on a tiny
tree frog. Tropical forests support huge populations of tree frogs, most of
which are active in the trees at night and easily located by predatory bats.*

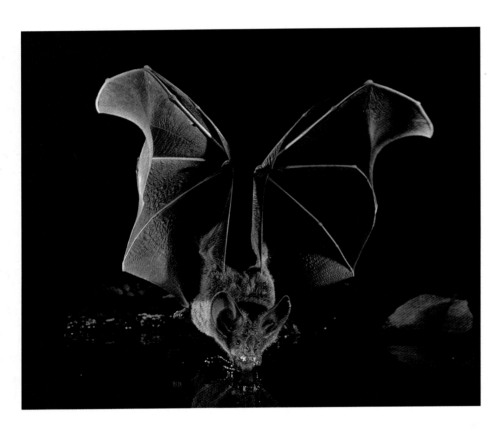

Most bats obtain water from their food, but they will sometimes swoop low over water to drink. This frog eating bat from Panama is keeping its wings up to avoid wetting them while drinking.

Even in summer in temperate regions, there will be periods of bad weather when feeding is not possible. If the energy expended in keeping warm, remaining active, and searching for food is not replenished by the food actually obtained, then it is dangerous to go out searching. The best thing to do is to become inactive and use up as little energy as possible. Bats have an excellent strategy for saving energy in these conditions. They can enter a torpid state where their body temperature drops to almost the same temperature as their surroundings, and their heart beat and rate of respiration slow down to an absolute minimum. If weather conditions become colder, their body temperature drops accordingly, and other bodily functions slow down as well. Bats can remain in this condition for weeks on end if weather conditions do not improve. Bats in this state look as if they are sleeping very soundly, but they can be awoken by a rise in temperature or sometimes by sudden noises.

When conditions are suitable, the bats will start to wake up. The first visible sign of this is shivering; this is thought to help the warming up process by making the muscles active and thus generating heat. At the same time, the breathing rate and heart start to speed up. The body temperature can rise by about 1.8° F (1°) C every minute, so it can sometimes take about 20 minutes to regain its full mobility and be able to fly. This is a very valuable strategy for saving energy, and bats will often enter torpor during the daytime in summer, even if the weather is not especially bad.

Winter time in temperate regions is not a good time for bats to find food. Since few insects are active then, bats would waste a great deal of energy in trying to hunt. Insect-eating birds have the option of migrating to warmer climates, but bats generally remain close to home and enter a more prolonged

Drinking

Most bats obtain some water from their food, but they will need to drink as well. They take water by swooping close to the surface of ponds and taking small sips as they fly past. Quite small bodies of water can be used, and bats have also been seen dipping over swimming pools; the effects of chlorinated water on the bats have not been studied, but some have been seen to do this on repeated evenings without any obvious ill effects. Some species will sip droplets of water from the roofs of caves, and others will take raindrops from large leaves.

Hibernation

In tropical regions, where food is available throughout the year and where the temperature remains high all the time, bats have no problem remaining active all year. In temperate regions, however, there are long periods of the year when food is not available. The summer glut of insects provides them with a short period when they must feed, grow, and reproduce. For the rest of the year, the most sensible thing to do is to save energy and hide out in a safe place.

A little brown bat collects condensation on its fur as it hibernates in a cave. During hibernation, the bat's metabolism slows down to such an extent that it becomes completely torpid, and its body temperature is almost the same as its surroundings.

A colony of greater horseshoe bats hibernate deep in a cave. Bats are vulnerable at this stage in their lives, so secure cave roosts are extremely important to their survival. They may spend several months in a state of torpor, protected from harsh winter weather in the stable environment of a cave.

period of hibernation. In the extremities of their range, winter hibernation may last, on and off, for about six months.

Prior to hibernation it is essential that the bats increase their body weight and build up fat reserves to see them through this very long period without food. Some species of hibernators have been known to increase their body weight by as much as 35 percent in this important run-up to winter. Even in a torpid state they will still need a reserve of energy to keep their bodily functions going, and since the activities of their bodies continue, but at a slower pace, they will wake up from time to time in order to get rid of wastes.

Hibernation sites have to be carefully chosen. They must be secure from predators, since during hibernation, the bats are completely inactive and unable to defend themselves at all. There must be a constant low temperature and a fairly high humidity. Sites that provide all of these conditions are few and far between, so those that are suitable are often used by very large numbers of bats. Natural caves are the best sites, but man-made sites like mine-shafts, tunnels, cellars, and large stone buildings may also be used.

If the temperature changes by more than a few degrees during the winter, the bats will need to move. If it is too warm, they will move to a cooler position so as not to waste stored body fat for energy by keeping their system running at a high rate. If it is too cold, they will also suffer and may not be able to survive prolonged periods below freezing. Wooden nesting boxes, frequently used in the summer for breeding and as summer roosts, are no good in winter as they are usually too exposed. Weak winter sun may warm them up too much and freezing conditions may prove fatal, so it is the more stable conditions of caves and similar sites which are usually chosen.

Bats will need to drink from time to time in winter, so the humidity of the hibernation site is critical to bats. Even though they are breathing very slowly, they still lose moisture from their lungs; in a very dry atmosphere this would occur more rapidly, necessitating more forays in search of water. Most bats store enough fat reserves to arouse themselves about five times during the course of the winter, but any more activity than this could leave them without enough reserves to last until food becomes available in the summer. Very mild spells may cause them to wake up and even venture out in search of food, although this is risky as there may be very little available. Bats can sometimes be seen feeding during the day in winter time; there are few species of winter gnats and winter moths that could provide a meal, but the chances of replenishing the energy used in searching for the food are very slight.

The ideal temperature for winter hibernation is somewhere between 32° F (0° C) and 59° F (15° C), and as winter progresses, the colder sites are used. Each bat will be aware of a number of sites within its home range and will be able to move from site to site according to the weather conditions. Some species will use hollow trees and holes in walls, but when conditions become very cold they will move to deeper hibernation sites where they are more protected.

In very cold weather the heart beat will slow down to about 25 beats a minute; for a bat this is very slow as the normal rate when flying is nearer to 1,000 beats a minute. The body temperature will be very close to that of the surroundings, and the bat will feel cold to the touch, but will not feel dead. However, bats should not be handled or disturbed in any way during hibernation as they wake up very easily and waste valuable energy.

During hibernation the bats are immobile for much of the time. Their breathing movements are gentle, and occasionally their feet may move to reach a more secure perch. Some species can open their mouths and make threatening calls, but they are easily awoken by lights and harsh noises, so winter hibernation sites must never be disturbed. Activities such as caving need to be controlled in sites where there are known to be bat roosts.

When better weather returns in the spring, bats face one of the most difficult periods in their lives. Their food reserves are almost entirely used up, so they must find food. Spring weather in temperate areas is notoriously unreliable. They may be lucky and experience mild, settled conditions, but there may be prolonged cold and wet spells when few insects are on the wing; this is when many bats will die. Those that do find food will still spend long periods in torpor, conserving their energy until the warmer days of summer arrive.

Roosting Sites

Roosting is the term used to describe the resting behavior of bats. When they are not flying in search of food they need a safe place to sleep and carry out other functions, such as grooming and caring for their young. Bats do not use any form of nesting material; they rely on their fur for insulation and seek out natural crevices and ledges to give them support and shelter. Most species will use a number of different roosts to provide them with the conditions they need through the year.

One of the many popular misconceptions about bats is that they inhabit drafty, cobweb-festooned garrets in old castles, or live among the bells in church towers. Bats generally do

Bats normally make no form of nest, but an exception to this is the tent-making bat of Central America. This fruit-eater folds palm fronds around itself for protection from tropical storms and predators.

not like belfries. Usually they are very drafty, having open louvers to allow the sounds of the pealing bells to ring out, and they are, by their very nature, incredibly noisy at times. No bat can tolerate the sounds of a peal of bells in full swing.

Like us, they enjoy a little comfort, so conditions like these would be avoided at all costs. More bats live in modern houses than crumbling old ruins; they like their breeding sites to be clean and safe.

Trees are important as roosts for many species; many of the flying foxes will hang from the branches of trees, wrapping their wings around them for protection from sudden tropical storms. The tent building bats wrap leaves around themselves for protection, biting through the midribs to make the leaves easier to fold. Smaller insectivorous species will use tree holes and crevices, or squeeze themselves behind loose bark. Tree roosts are very difficult to find in some areas because so many old, decaying trees are cut down and never replaced.

A palm tree in Mataranka in Australia's Northern Territory is used as a communal roost by a large group of little red flying foxes.

A group of black flying foxes from the Eungella National Park, Queensland, Australia, roost on open branches, their large wings wrapped around them to protect them from sudden rainstorms.

A heliconia leaf makes a rain-proof tent for these white tent-making bats from Costa Rica. The bats bite through the ribs of the leaves making them easier to fold over, and giving them a few rough places to hold on to.

Bats often live in very large colonies; where suitable roosts are scarce they compete for space and the best sites are often very crowded. A cave in Mexico serves as a safe nursery for a large group of young Mexican free-tailed bats. In some colonies, it has been estimated that up to 50 million bats could be living there at one time.

Many bats live in houses; often the human inhabitants are quite unaware of their small lodgers, and only very occasionally discover them when climbing into the roof space, or if they happen to see them leaving the roost at night. Gaining access to suitable roosting spaces can be a problem to bats. Modern houses tend to be very well built with few gaps for the bats to enter. Some of the smaller species will squeeze themselves in through the tiniest gaps such as spaces between tiles and crevices made by warped planks or timbers. Some bats will remain in tiny crevices, but others will move around in the loft space until they find somewhere suitable. Clean, dry, draft-proof sites are preferred, and if suitable conditions are found, large numbers of bats may congregate there.

Many bats are very small, and when roosting communally, they are happy to live in very close proximity to each other. If bats are seen emerging, it is possible to count them, but sometimes they use several exits and estimating how many are present can be difficult. Some of the larger bats, such as the horseshoe bats prefer the cellar to the attic, but will still need easy access in the form of a broken window or grating. On rare occasions, a bat will

find its way into the domestic quarters of a house; it is usually lost and frantically trying to find its way out. Leaving a window open is normally sufficient for it to make its escape, but sometimes it will settle on a wall or the curtains and can then be carefully covered with a soft cloth and taken outside to be released. There may be problems if the bat flies around a room with a security alarm in it, as they have been known to trigger them off.

Artificial bat roosts can take a variety of bats. Many of the tree-roosters will use bat boxes if they are positioned correctly, and access can be provided into roof spaces to allow them to enter easily. Boards attached to the walls of a house, high up under the eaves, will also be readily used if they are fitted in such a way that gaps are left between them.

Sometimes bats roosting in a building may cause problems by depositing their droppings in an inconvenient place. If they are roosting in the high rafters of a church, for example, droppings may fall onto worshippers below. Most bat droppings are dry and consist of little more than insect wing cases, but droppings containing fruit remains may be more troublesome. The bats can usually be persuaded to move away from the roost by covering access

Bats accomodate themselves very well to roosting in buildings. In fact, the snugness and cleanliness of modern structures is appealing to them. Here, a group of little brown bats has taken up residence in th roof of a farmer's shed.

FOLLOWING PAGE: Long-nosed bats from Costa Rica cling to a branch in the forest prior to making feeding forays in the upper canopy.

55

holes or the roost itself. Take care that no bat protection laws are infringed by interfering with the bats or their roost.

Bats are not found only in open country or in gardens; there are plenty of opportunities for them in cities. For one thing, there is usually no shortage of roosting sites; city parks often have large trees, and there are a good range of buildings and other man-made structures to choose from. There may not be quite the number of insects in the city, but street lighting concentrates those that do occur into smaller areas; also lakes and ponds are good sources of night-flying insects. Temperatures in towns are often a few degrees higher than in the countryside, so the periods of activity may be longer.

The droppings that accumulate under a roost are usually dry and inoffensive, but bat urine may be more of a problem if large numbers

of bats habitually roost in the same part of a building. In some parts of the world where bats roost in the millions, the droppings accumulate to such an extent that they can be collected by the ton and used as a fertilizer.

Emergence

Emergence can be a most spectacular event when hundreds of thousands of bats are involved. Watching the dusk sky darken as a chattering throng of bats streams out of a cave is a never-to-be-forgotten wildlife spectacle. However, even the emergence of a few dozen bats from a tree hole can prove to be an interesting event.

Audible squeaking and chattering usually precedes emergence. Sometimes a whole colony will emerge in rapid succession. On other occasions, a few at a time will venture out, while others will think better of it and stay inside. Sometimes roost-watching can be most unproductive as no bats emerge at all, either as a result of bad weather, or because the whole colony has decided to move off to another area. The timing of emergence can usually be predicted and is normally linked to the time of sunset. In equatorial regions, this is at the same time almost every day, but in temperate regions the timing of nightfall is quite variable; of course, in winter, there will be no emergence at all. Emergence should be followed later on by a return to the roost after a night's foraging; females with young to suckle may return fairly soon, but others may stay out nearly all night, returning shortly before dawn to groom and then sleep.

Some predators have learnt that the mass emergence of bats from a known roost can provide them with an easy meal. Domestic cats are a serious problem in some urban areas, since they can sit on the roof and catch small bats with ease as they emerge from their roost in a building. In more natural sites, some birds of prey have learnt to hunt in the near darkness and will take a few bats each night.

Mexican free-tail bats often live in immense colonies, where the numbers present may exceed tens of millions. The sky darkens as they leave their roosts, and the sound of their flapping wings and chattering calls can be heard from a great distance.

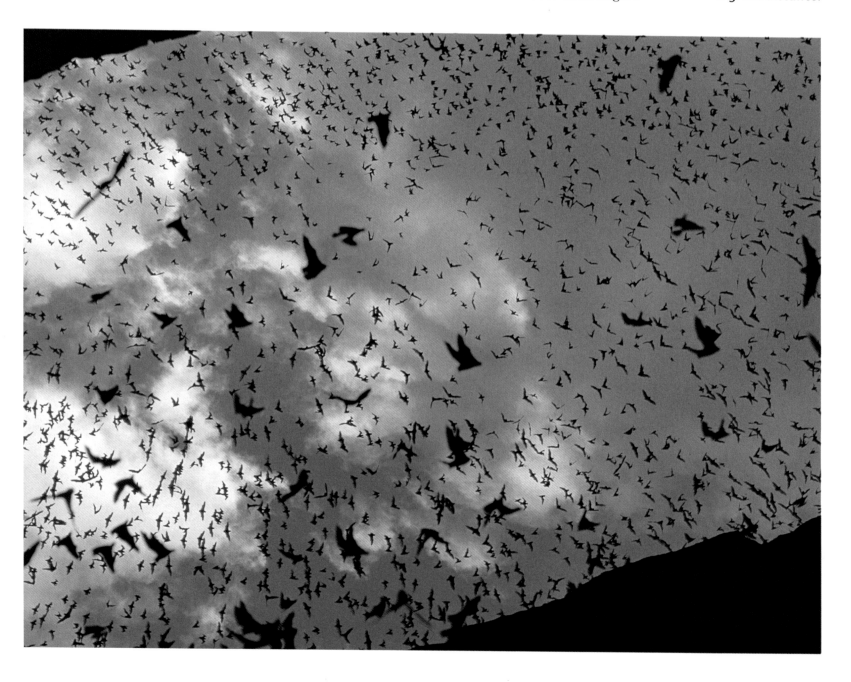

A fringe-lipped bat makes a surprise attack on a frog, swooping silently down on its prey and seizing it in its mouth. The teeth are sharp and needle-like for piercing the prey's skin, and the jaws powerful enough to grip it tightly as the bat flies away.

Bats have exploited many sources of food, and some species are adept at catching fish at night. Surface-feeding fish can be detected by the faint ripples they make at the surface, and are caught in the bats' extended hind feet which have long powerful claws.

A frog-eating bat from Barro Colorado Island, Panama, has returned to its roost with its prey so that it can begin to swallow it. A large frog is usually killed by a bite to the head

FAMILIES AND COLONIES

For bats in temperate climates, mating usually takes place in the autumn or winter, but fertilization does not occur until the following spring; the female will carry the sperm inside her, and only after she has successfully emerged from hibernation will she ovulate and stimulate fertilization. The embryo will then begin to develop, but the rate at which this happens is dependent on temperature and food availability. If the female is torpid for long periods due to cold weather or lack of food, the embryo will develop very slowly.

Caring for the Young

In warm weather, the female will use roost sites that are warm during the day, thus speeding up the development rate of the embryo.

Many females will roost together, further increasing the temperature. The young will be born into these females-only groups in summer, the actual date depending on the variable length of pregnancy. Some nursery colonies will contain many hundreds of bats with their babies, and they can be very noisy, with a constant clamor of chattering and squeaking. In most species the females produce only one baby a year, but there are exceptions, and some species can produce twins or even triplets.

The birth process is not easy for a species that hangs upside down, so some bats will turn themselves upright in order to ease the birth. The tail membrane is usually used to cradle the baby when it is first born. It is then encouraged to crawl along the underside of the mother to find one of the two teats located on either side of the chest. The mother will use one of her wings to help hold the baby in place until it learns to grip on properly for itself. Baby bats are quite large in proportion

Communal roosting is a feature of many bats. Heat is conserved when large numbers roost in close proximity, and humidity is maintained at a high level.

A female red bat cradles her offspring. The young bat instinctively clings to the mother's fur, but she must also take care that it does not drop to the ground. Unusually for bats, red bats sometimes produce twins, or even three offspring in one litter.

Bats are caring parents and have evolved methods of feeding and protecting of their young that are in harmony with their unusual, airborne lifestyle. Here, a Mexican free-tailed mother is nursing her baby.

A newly-born gray bat has been left by its mother to cling to the roof of the nursery cave. Young bats are normally hairless and blind when first born, and totally dependent on their mothers for food and warmth. They are left in a safe place while the mother seeks food.

to the size of the mother, some of them weighing almost a quarter of the mother's weight.

When first born, the babies are pink and hairless, but gradually soft gray hair grows, and they begin to look a little more like bats. The eyes are closed at birth, and it is not until the babies are about a week old that the eyes open. Growth is rapid for the first week or two on a diet of mothers' milk. The babies have milk teeth, but do not need them for feeding; they are used more for hanging on to the mother's fur. The toes and thumbs are also essential for gripping the mother, as she is quite likely to carry the baby around with her sometimes, especially if changing to a new roosting site. When the babies have grown their first coat of fur and the eyes are fully open, the mothers will leave them in nursery areas while they go off to feed, returning periodically to suckle them during the night.

Individuals recognize their own babies by their unique calls and scents.

When they are about three weeks old the young will probably be large enough to venture out with the adults on short flights. They will still be suckling at this stage, but they will be learning about their territory and how to find the way back to their roosts. It will take a few more weeks before they are able to start feeding for themselves.

Most small bat species are mature enough to breed in their second year, but larger ones may not breed until their third or fourth year. Not all of the females in a colony will breed every year. There are various reasons why they may not do this: They may have failed to find a mate, or lost their young at a very early stage, or they may be infertile. Producing young, that are one-quarter of the mother's own body weight, requires considerable levels of stamina

A young fruit bat takes its first flight under the wing of its mother. Although still suckling at this stage, it will be taken to good sources of food in order to learn more about its surroundings.

and fitness in female bats. A poor feeding season prior to the winter's hibernation may sometimes leave the bats in too weak a condition to support a developing embryo.

Male bats play little part in breeding apart from mating. Many species show a high degree of promiscuity, with males mating with as many females as possible. Once mating is over, the bats will roost communally for the winter. In spring, the members of a bat colony will separate. The females will choose a safe nursery area for the birth of their babies, and the males will disperse to smaller colonies, or perhaps roost singly.

Bat Society

Bats are often found in very large colonies, with some species congregating in staggering numbers; roosts counted in millions are not unknown. Even the scarcest species form colonies, even though they may number only a few individuals.

In winter, roosts tend to be communal affairs, with all sexes and ages sharing the same site, but during the breeding season, females will seek out warmer sites for the birth of their young. Non-breeding females may remain with them, but males will be elsewhere. Some bats form mixed colonies where roosting sites are large enough and there is sufficient food nearby. Counting bats at roosts and establishing which species are present is very difficult, since they may move several times during the course of the summer. On rainy nights they may not emerge at all, and on other nights, some of the population may move to another location, leaving the others behind. What all this indicates is that bats are highly mobile mammals who can explore their environment and make the best use of the resources available to them. Behavior varies between species, with some species being highly mobile, exploring a large area in search of food and safe roosting sites, while others are more sedentary, rarely straying far from night to night.

The tropical species, that are not faced with the necessity of hibernating, simply need to find food. If that food consists of fruit or nectar, nightly forays are made from the roosting site over a wide area. Tree roosters may eventually kill their tree with their droppings, leaving them exposed through lack of foliage; this will force them to move to a more sheltered site.

FOLLOWING PAGE: A young fruit bat soon develops the facial features typical of its mother, including the long tongue needed for feeding on fruits and flowers.

A female Natterer's bat, a common European species, cares for her helpless newborn baby. Young bats are tended by their mothers for several weeks, and are brooded while they are still hairless.

When a tree is habitually used by a large colony of fruit bats, the accumulation of their acidic droppings can kill off the foliage, making the bats rather conspicuous. They will eventually seek another, more secure roosting tree.

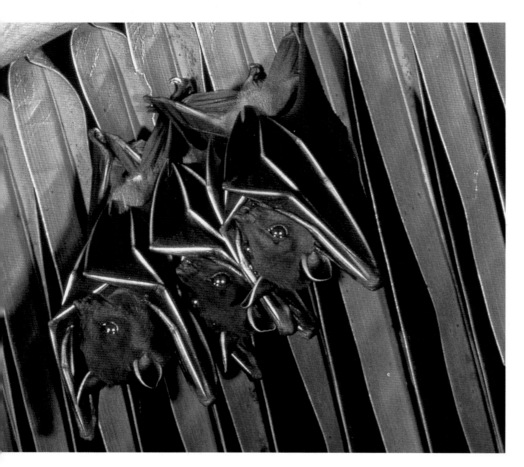

A trio of greater short-nosed fruit bats hang from a palm frond in a forest in Thailand. Deforestation on a grand scale has greatly reduced the areas of natural habitat left for these species, so they are increasingly found in areas of cultivation.

Bats and the Law

In many countries bats are protected species, and it is an offense to harm them or their roosts. Special permission is needed to carry out research on them, and regulations apply to such activities as repairing the roofs of houses that are known to have bat roosts in them. Providing nesting boxes for bats is permitted, but opening the boxes to have a look inside is not.

Bat Conservation

Bats, like many other creatures, are in need of special protection in many areas. They have their natural predators and diseases, but these are not endangering populations; they have always been present. Bats face serious threats through the loss of their habitat to deforestation, intensification of agriculture, the spread of cities and industrial sites, and the increasing use of pesticides. Lack of food and consumption of food that has been contaminated by pesticides are serious problems and can lead to poor breeding success.

Secure roosting sites are crucial to the survival of bats, especially those species that need to hibernate. Deforestation destroys their tree roosts, and mining and quarrying can damage caves. The increasing use of caves for recreation disturbs important roosts in areas of high human population. Bats frequently use human habitation for roosting and find some modern homes ideal, but they are likely to come into contact with domestic cats which are serious predators in some areas.

Bats are inoffensive creatures that cause no problems to humans. Indeed, they are often beneficial in that they consume huge numbers of potentially harmful insects, or act as the principal pollinators of fruit-bearing trees and shrubs. They also aid seed dispersal in a large number of tropical tree species. In some parts of the world, large species are hunted by humans for food, or they may be taken for some supposed medical benefits. They are not capable of damaging houses by gnawing into woodwork as mice or rats can, for example, and the only problem that might occur is an accumulation of droppings in some favored roost sites. Bats are scrupulously clean, spending a long time grooming each day to rid their fur of parasites, so they can not be considered a threat to health.

Most of the so-called problems that arise when bats share human habitation come from a lack of understanding of these small, but fascinating mammals. The more we understand about bats, the better equipped we will be to safeguard their future.

The common pipistrelle is one of Europe's smallest bats. It is quite likely to be found in towns, and frequently roosts in houses. Though it is tempting for people to take a close look at these creatures, they should be aware that there are laws in many countries protecting bats from being disturbed.

INDEX

*Page numbers in **bold-face** type indicate photo captions.*